I Just Can't Ducking Pump Anymore

A Mindset Shift for Moms Who Struggle with Supply

Sarah Farrell Johnson

I Just Can't Ducking Pump Anymore
A Mindset Shift for Moms Who Struggle with Supply

Copyright © 2019 Sarah Farrell Johnson

All rights reserved. This book or parts thereof may not be reproduced in any form, stored in any retrieval system, or transmitted in any form by any means — electronic, mechanical, photocopy, recording, or otherwise — without prior written permission of the publisher, except as provided by The United States of America copyright law. For permission requests, write to the publisher at:

www.facebook.com/ijustcantf
or
mindsetshiftjohnson@gmail.com

The author of this book does not dispense medical advice or prescribe the use of any technique as a form of treatment for physical or medical problems without the advice of a physician or lactation consultant, either directly or indirectly. The intent of the author is only to offer information of a general nature to help you in your quest for emotional and spiritual well-being. In the event you use any of the information in this book for yourself, which is your constitutional right, the author and the publisher assume no responsibility for your actions.

Cover by Tamara Burden
Back cover photograph by Alex Perez @a2eorigins
Interior formatting by Dave Scott

ISBN: 9781075480607

First printing June 2019

DEDICATION

For my husband Brian, who always encourages me to follow my dreams and hangs on for the ride.

For my daughter Allie, may you be blessed with perfect breasts (ha!)

For my son Micah, for taking this journey with me.

For Sarah S., who has provided millions of ounces of love for Micah.

For Mary R., Lacy B., and Tamara B. for your edits and talents.

For all women who donate milk to other moms. You give a divine gift.

For anyone who has the courage to have a breast reduction.

For all breastfeeding mammas: past, present, and future.

For all seeking enlightenment and well-being.

CONTENTS

- INTRODUCTION 1
- CHAPTER 1 – Breast Reductions Are a Mardi Gras Nightmare 5
- CHAPTER 2 – Becoming Mamma 9
- CHAPTER 3 – Obsessed with Production 17
- CHAPTER 4 – A Love-Centered Perspective 21
- CHAPTER 5 – Self Coaching Model 27
- CHAPTER 6 – Using the Self Coaching Model 41
- CHAPTER 7 – A Thought Framework for Breastfeeding Issues 49
- CHAPTER 8 – Sustaining New thoughts and Goals 69
- CHAPTER 9 – Ending the Adventure 77
- CHAPTER 10 – My Desires Came True 81
- CHAPTER 11 – Summary: The Mindset-Allowing-Action Process 83
- CHAPTER 12 – Love to All Mammas 89
- CHAPTER 13 – My Favorite Resources 93
- REFERENCES 97
- ABOUT THE AUTHOR 99

INTRODUCTION

This book came about as a response to my personal struggle as a BFAR mom. (BFAR means breastfeeding after a reduction.) In connecting with many other BFAR moms in our Facebook group, it seems to be a common theme for us to stress about not being able to have enough supply to feed our babies. Most of us have tried it all — herbs, power pumping, Domperidone® medications, diet changes, overeating, lactation cookies, beverages, and more, in an effort to produce milk for our babies. The heartbreak, grief, stress, and self-battering that I have read (again and again) via posts in our Facebook group propelled me to write this book to speak to everyone who is in pain and conflict over their breastfeeding journeys.

Although most BFAR moms struggle with a special type of frustration or even guilt, the idea of not producing enough milk to feed our babies fully is not unique to just BFAR moms. There are many moms who also have a low supply for reasons out of their control. Some moms never started with enough from the beginning; some lost milk when they returned to work, got sick, or decided to go on a diet. Some were not educated enough about how to take care of their supply. There are a multitude of amazing mothers facing this issue.

If you are looking for a book with an exhaustive list of what you can do to up your supply, this is not it. There are many of those books available, information online, and valuable conversations and resources through Internationally Certified Board Lactation Consultants (IBCLCs). There are also lots of products marketed at you (think lactation cookies, lactation protein powders, etc.) to help you up your supply or make money off of your insecurities. Instead, this book proposes a mindset shift for you to feel comfortable with the amazing gift that you are able to give your baby, no matter how much or how little.

Here's the truth that you need to hear if you're struggling with breastfeeding: you don't need to be able to provide a full supply of milk for your baby to breastfeed. You don't even need to supply half. You don't even have to supply a quarter. Anytime that babe is on your boob, you're breastfeeding. Period. Even if baby is refusing the boob and you're exclusively pumping for him, you're a breastfeeding mamma.

Think about that for a second. You don't need to exclusively breastfeed to breastfeed.

It took me a long time to accept that I was a breastfeeding mom even though I supplemented with formula and donated breast milk. After months of trying everything to up my supply and stressing myself in the process, my body seemed to settle on producing about four ounces a day. FOUR! "Not even close enough," I told myself.

For someone who is in the midst of struggling, we don't feel like we have enough milk, or do enough, or are good enough moms as we try to feed our babies. We don't feel like providers. By changing our mindset, however, and viewing our situation as someone who is breastfeeding, no matter what the supply may be, we can find love and clarity to replace our negative feelings. Someone who

INTRODUCTION

hasn't had a breast reduction, or who can maybe supply more than half of the baby's daily needs, or who doesn't breastfeed at all, would probably tell you this truth very easily: you are already a breastfeeding mom, and whatever you can produce is good enough. If you are feeding your baby on or from the breast at all, you're breastfeeding and you're a success!

Let that sink in for a second. You are already a success. If you don't feel that way right now, wouldn't you like to feel that way? It is up to you to tap into that feeling. If you felt like you were already doing what you intended to, you'd realize you have already met your goal. And if you have already met your goal with breastfeeding, why are you struggling with avenues like power pumping, herbs, etc.? What if you believed that you already do enough, and you already are enough just the way you are? What might the rest of your breastfeeding journey feel like and look like?

This book will propose a mindset shift for you to relieve the pressure you have needlessly put on yourself. It's a forgiving mindset shift that comes from a place of loving yourself unconditionally. It is a new beginning, a fresh start, a letting go of thoughts that no longer serve you, and a welcoming of those that will. It isn't about throwing your pump away, but it is about finding the path that honors you. I challenge you to read my story and apply the new thought processes to your breastfeeding journey and see what happens. You may just have the happiest relationship with yourself and your baby that you've ever had.

CHAPTER 1

BREAST REDUCTIONS ARE A MARDI GRAS NIGHTMARE

I had a breast reduction when I was 18 because I was insecure about my breasts. I thought they were saggy, very saggy, too saggy. I thought my nipples were too big. "Ew! No one likes big nipples," I convinced myself. I was horrified to be intimate with the many men that wanted to experience the "hot big-chested blonde." I felt pretty with clothes on but with clothes off, I was insecure. And to be fair, my shoulders hurt — a lot. I was a great, lean weight from soccer and the boobs just took over my whole frame — along with my ability to love my body, or so I thought.

If I could go back in time, knowing what I know now, I might have tried physical therapy first. Maybe I should have strengthened my back and shoulders, and simply found some strong role models to assure me that everyone is insecure about something on their body at that age. (Hell, I still am — hello, leftover baby belly!) And the joke really is on me because with the surgery I had, I not only have scars on my breasts (anchor and around the nipple), but because of the way the surgery needed to be performed for my anatomy, I have leftover areola underneath my new nipples. Yes, I have dark, nipple-colored areas underneath my current nipples! Buh-bye bucket list Mardi Gras trip! (My dad must be relieved somewhere in the afterlife...)

In effect, the surgery only sort-of cured what I was looking to fix. I was still super self-conscious about my breasts every time I had a new partner in my 20s in the same way that I was worried about having "big nipples" back in my teens. Surgery didn't change my insecurities. Thought work and accepting self-love changes them. It took getting married in my 30s to finally drop this self-flagellation about the breasts I was born with. I guess I finally just hit a point where I was ready to believe that I could be beautiful while naked with my weird scars. Thanks, hubby.

Do I regret my decision to have a breast reduction? Mostly no, only a tad yes. No, because I am grateful that I've had over a decade of smaller, perky breasts. I've really enjoyed being able to fit bras — strapless bras! — and choose shirts that weren't popping buttons off the top, or too baggy at the waist to accommodate my obtuse triangle torso. I loved being able to choose bathing suits without needing to buy the top two sizes up, and I finally felt like I could "hide" and not draw so much sexual attention. I could finally be more "normal" like everyone else, like my gorgeous best friend Rachel. We could wear tube tops together. (Ha! Think 1998!) I also loved being able to long distance run and fit in a real sports bra.

However, with my first baby, the complications that came with breastfeeding seemed insurmountable and I ended up giving up entirely. I imagine that if you are picking up this book then you may be toying with some of the same emotions I experienced. Will I be able to feed

CHAPTER 1 – BREAST REDUCTIONS ARE A MARDI GRAS NIGHTMARE

her? Will she be able to latch? Even if she can, what if nothing comes out? What if I don't make enough milk to feed her? Is it even worth it to try to breastfeed if I have to formula-feed her afterwards anyway? Is formula really okay for babies? This takes up so much time for such a little amount of milk that I produce. Do I even want to risk undoing my perky, post-surgery breasts?

It's important that we start choosing thoughts that serve us, no matter what point we are in our breastfeeding journey. I'm assuming that most of you are at the point where you've tried everything possible to breastfeed and have exhausted yourself and your possibilities of upping your supply. That is where I was too, and then I started doing the mindset shift that I will discuss in this book to help not only lower my stress, but change my demeanor entirely.

Maybe you are picking up this book before you've given birth, which is even better. It will be great for you to give breastfeeding your all while having this thought work in place.

Wherever you are in your breastfeeding journey, I can't wait to share with you the thoughts that have served me, my family, and my baby boy. I went from completely giving up on breastfeeding my first-born girl at four weeks to breastfeeding my son seven months happily with the couple ounces a day (or less) that my body can make.

CHAPTER 2

BECOMING MAMMA

I share my story in hopes that parts of it will resonate with each of you. I have one girl, Allison, who is now three, and one boy, Micah (pronounced like MY-kuh) who is less than a year old. Because of my mindset shifts regarding birth plans and breastfeeding, I have had two very different experiences with each of my children.

Allie's Story

When my first baby, Allison (Allie), was born, I had a pretty neutral vibe going into the breastfeeding scene, although I was worried I might not be able to produce due to my reduction. Frankly, I didn't really read much about breastfeeding besides looking up a few positions in which to hold the baby and ordering my pump through my insurance. "Why would it be hard to breastfeed?" I thought. "People have been giving birth and breastfeeding for millions of years…" While I was pregnant, I didn't research the benefits and I honestly didn't give it much thought and didn't care if I ended up giving my baby formula due to my breast reduction.

Well, I created my own reality. My daughter was formula-fed her whole first year of life and I did not stick with breastfeeding past four weeks. She also endured some incurable constipation from figuring out the right formula. The struggle and guilt were terrible.

Quick disclaimer: I am not saying that formula isn't awesome. Oh, it is. And thank God for it or my daughter wouldn't be healthy, smart, bilingual, and on the 90th percentile of the height charts. Formula saved my ass. Let's not get into this stupid debate about *Breast is Best* vs. *Fed is Best*. There's no politics here. You do what you need to do to feed your baby, and we all know that breast milk is great, otherwise you wouldn't be reading this. And if you are already formula feeding or end up formula feeding exclusively, good for you. Okay, disclaimer over.

We can quickly fall into the pit when we start on a downward spiral, giving up breastfeeding or letting our negative thoughts impact our decision-making abilities. This certainly happened to me. It's critical that we have our spirit and mind in a high-flying place in order to see any type of results. This comes from work: thought work.

I wanted and expected to have an all-natural birth with Allie. Once again, I didn't really do any type of preparation and just figured that I was a strong-willed person who has endured a lot of pain before, and it would suck, but I'd make it through. (After all, I cut my friggin' boobs off, right?) Of course, I was wrong. Really wrong. Allie's birth did not end up how I desired; I'm not going to get into the full birth story, but let's sum it up: I ended up very disheartened after getting a ride on the conveyor belt that is Pitocin > epidural > episiotomy.

Twenty-eight hours. Yep, I'm super grateful for that epidural now, but it wasn't how I wanted it. And it came with a whole array of negative thoughts that started my spiral into a year of much more frustration, anger, and sadness than I should have been experiencing. From my view of what felt like a "disaster birth" sprung more negative thoughts that tanked my breastfeeding. It was a year where I didn't hold onto the good moments. I wished many moments would fast-forward, more moments than I care to admit, praying time would just heal my wounds and that things would ease up and being mommy would be easier.

I believe wholeheartedly, knowing what I know now, that if I'd had a clear vision for Allie's birth and babyhood, if I had meditated on it, and if I'd had better thought patterns and coping mechanisms and been better educated, then my birth, my breastfeeding, and my first year as a mom would have been much more fun.

***

I entered motherhood with the energy and belief that so much was out of my control, starting with the thought that I was powerless and "weak" for getting the epidural. I cannot stress enough that this isn't true, but that was my thought reality at the time. Combine that attitude with the seemingly endless sleepless nights of a newborn, and all the new skills which moms must quickly obtain; my spiral just continued to sink as I pumped and pumped and pumped and saw less than 15 ml of milk per pump session.

My thoughts began to go something like this:

"What is the point of doing this if I only get a tiny amount?"

"This will never feed her."

"My supply isn't increasing."

"I'm so sick of pumping. All I do is pump."

"At least with the bottle I'm getting more sleep, and Brian can wake up to feed her too."

"JUST LATCH ALREADY... come on, that's not how you do it."

"How does a baby not know how to latch?"

"GOD DAMN SNS! Now, she doesn't even want my nipple anymore... she just sucks the tube."

"This is stupid."

"It's obvious that I can't breastfeed, and I have to go back to work in two weeks. Pumping this tiny amount is not even worth my time at work to pump."

"Ugh, okay. Let's just do 100% formula. This just isn't worth it."

Giving up on breastfeeding only furthered my sour mindset. I felt like a failure, like I didn't have the strength to give my all to her. Other negative feelings followed as her infancy continued, like taking beautiful newborn pictures with her and smiling, exhausted, hoping to appear as a happy new mom, when I really cared more about her sleeping through the night (damnit!). Or, being so exasperated with being a new mom that I was happy to return to work at six weeks and get a break from her. It meant that I could avoid the fact that I was failing as a mom, if only for eight hours. I could have *some* sense of freedom back, and feel more like myself. Worst of all, I felt guilty for the tiny bit of relief that it provided.

How did I snap myself out of my spiral? One day I woke up and realized that I wasn't enjoying being a mom the way I thought I would, and since I didn't want to trade in my kid, I'd better step it up and start having some type of fun. It was almost her first birthday and the days had gone by so fast.

Had I empowered myself to change my thought patterns sooner, she probably would have been breastfed. My second baby, Micah, is breastfed. It's too bad I waited almost an entire year to decide to start changing my thoughts, because the truth is, we have the power to change them at any point to allow ourselves to be happy.

When things are not going how we want them to, we can choose frustration, or we can choose joy. We have so much more power than we realize, and if we let our minds go on default mode — experiencing feelings instead of intentionally choosing them — then we will end up having our lives lived by decisions made from frustration, instead of lives we desired from choices we made from joy.

Micah's Story

After gaining some important life experience from having my daughter, I wanted my entire birth and feeding situation to be different with Micah. First, let me say, that my mindset was so sour with Allie that when people asked me, "Aww, are you going to have another one?" my answer was, "No, no, no, she's going to be an only child." This was my answer for well over a year. There's nothing wrong with having only one child, but deep in my heart of hearts I had always envisioned my life with two children. So, for me to say this, it was obvious to close friends and family that I was very closed off.

I started to slowly change my mindset when Allie turned one. Her birthday took place in a building that was situated on a lake. After the party was over, my husband

and I walked out to the lake alone and sat on a bench which had an incredible view. It was crisp weather and being next to the water made me feel at peace. I can't recall if I actually started to cry aloud or not, but it was then that I decided to let go. I let go of all the guilt that I had held about everything I thought I didn't do right. I started to release my feelings of not being a good enough mom. I started to forgive myself — just a little bit — for some of the decisions that I had made out of frustration. I started to accept that maybe it needed to start being okay that I had given up on breastfeeding. I had ended an entire year not enjoying being a mom, and it was time to change that. I was finally ready to take on motherhood.

I'm not one hundred percent sure when I was ready to have number two, but January of 2018 we decided we would start trying to have another because we wanted a fall baby, and within two weeks I was pregnant again. I wanted everything about this pregnancy and onward to be different. I wanted to gain less weight, I wanted to have an un-medicated natural birth, and I wanted to breastfeed my baby. I attribute many of the successes that followed to a change in my thought patterns that helped make this happen.

My pregnancy with Micah was better. I am a runner, and I was not able to run with either pregnancy due to hip pain from the high impact. But with Micah, I saw a physical therapist and I was able to stave off some weight gain because I became strong enough to power walk. Even at 35 weeks pregnant, I was strong enough to power walk a 5k, with Allie in the stroller! My changed thoughts allowed me to receive help, which in turn made me stronger.

CHAPTER 2 – BECOMING MAMMA

To address having a natural birth, I changed my egocentric thought that I wouldn't need to read birthing books (women have been doing this for millions of years without books, right?) and buckled down and read all about natural births. I talked to friends who had done it. I surrounded myself with a support system, too. I hired a doula and she was such a gift to help me through the birthing process the way I had planned it. I successfully had a non-medicated, unassisted birth with my son, and it was awesome. Yes, it was painful, don't get me wrong (I begged for the epidural in the heat of it), but it was empowering and glorious.

And now, since I am doing my thought work regarding breastfeeding, I am breastfeeding my son. Can I exclusively breastfeed my son? No. Does that make me any less of a breastfeeding mom? I used to think so, but no. Does my success depend on how much I can produce? It did for a long time, but now it does not. I am finally at a stage where I feel like I am providing for my son, and meeting my goal of breastfeeding for him. More importantly, I am really enjoying being mamma.

Allison (3 years) & Micah (6 months)

CHAPTER 3

OBSESSED WITH PRODUCTION

How do you talk about yourself to others? About your breastfeeding situation? What types of thoughts are you thinking? Positive or negative? What types of feelings are arising due to those thoughts?

You see, the thing that tripped me up for a long time, and trips up most breastfeeding after a reduction (BFAR) moms is the idea that the goal is to exclusively be able to provide for your baby with your breast milk. Due to our surgeries, many of us are physically incapable of this production. So why would this be the only goal we have? We would bet setting ourselves up to fail.

When I first started feeding Micah, I went full force. I researched beforehand. I read *Defining Your Own Success* by Diana West. (I highly recommend the book, by the way, as it inspired me for my second breastfeeding journey and is very informative for BFAR mothers, and is very informative for professionals like IBCLCs as well.) I researched diets and herbs. I looked into and purchased multiple supplemental nursing systems (SNS). I filled an entire deep freezer with donated breast milk. You name it, I was ON IT! I had it covered. My son was getting breast milk, God damn it.

And after he was born, he latched after only practicing for a few days. I relaxed my mind and body this time. I saw a lactation consultant who gave me great tips. With Allie, I couldn't get her to latch because I was too frustrated. I kept forcing it and was so irritated and sad that she wasn't getting it. I didn't know what a good latch felt like and I thought I couldn't afford a lactation consultant. These limiting thoughts closed doors for me. It's easier to see in retrospect that it was me who was the problem, not her.

With Micah, I told myself that I would not be the person standing in my way this time. I wanted to continue breastfeeding for a year and try to exclusively breastfeed him. I was super encouraged when I started to see drops of colostrum and thrilled when milk came in. At first I could pump about 5-10 ml on each side. I kept him on the breast and used an SNS (Supplemental Nursing System). At one month, my supply jumped and I could pump half an ounce (15 ml) on each side or more. I was very happy. My morning pump was about 1-1.5 oz. (30-45 ml).

This is where my supply stayed, and where I started to stress a bit. I started to get off track with my thinking, and I wasn't even realizing it. After all, I hadn't been examining my thoughts. Who has time for that? (Ha!) My baby was a serious overeater. I mean, really, what kind of baby can drink six oz. every two hours at two weeks old?!

My supply wasn't changing and my deep freezer that held close to 4,000 ounces of donated breast milk was

CHAPTER 3 — OBSESSED WITH PRODUCTION

quickly diminishing. Around two months old, I realized he would probably be through all of it within the month, and I was correct. By three months old the milk was consumed and I started to freak out.

My thoughts started going something like this as I felt my nerves get slightly more and more on edge as the weeks passed:

"WTF, why am I not getting more milk?"

"I'm pumping every few hours. I'm doing everything right."

"What are we going to do when the milk runs out?!"

"I can't produce enough to feed him. He's going to need formula like Allie did, and he's going to end up constipated, too."

"I wonder if I should try power pumping."

"What! How does power pumping NOT give me more milk?"

"Maybe I should stop the goat's rue."

"I need to research some more herbs."

"Damn it, I am such a failure."

"I'm never going to be able to provide for my baby."

Many more thoughts like this plagued my mind and I fell into the struggle that a lot of BFAR moms do. I tried forcing an increase. I was willing to sacrifice and do almost anything. I tried power pumping. Hell, one time I was on a long car ride home and I pumped 10 minutes on 10 minutes off for seven times in a row. Then I power pumped for three days after that. I had some uterus pain, but nope, no more milk. I tried adding in more herbs. I took fenugreek: three capsules, three times a day, for a month. The websites said that you knew you took enough because you'd start to smell like maple syrup. I didn't. So

I upped it to four capsules. I added blessed thistle and milk thistle. I added liquid Legendairy Milk® supplements. I started eating foods that were supposed to promote breast milk: oatmeal, brewer's yeast, sunflower lecithin, barley, fennel, chickpeas, healthy fats, blue Gatorade®... can you guess what happened? My milk stayed the same and I was more stressed out, frustrated, and hopeless with each new approach that I tried.

I became resentful that nothing was working. I was irritated that I spent so much time hooked to my pump at work and home, but I was only producing an ounce or two. I felt like it was wasted time that could otherwise be spent more enjoyably. Instead of appreciating the sunlight during a walk on my lunch break, I sat and listened to the in-and-out *woosh* of the Medela® under the fluorescent lights of my classroom. At home, my hands were tied up, holding the flanges, and I was hooked to an outlet so I couldn't do things I needed to for my toddler. I hated how much effort I was putting into pumping for what felt like zero improvement.

CHAPTER 4

A LOVE-CENTERED PERSPECTIVE

Oftentimes, it is only after we have exhausted every other option that we find clarity. Around four months into breastfeeding, I realized that I'd had enough and wasn't going to continue in this manner anymore. I had learned from the last time that I didn't want to give up breastfeeding, but I felt stuck.

At first, I even felt selfish accepting donated breast milk from others when I wasn't willing to go overboard trying to up my supply anymore. But then, I thought to myself, "How is this honoring my family and me?" It wasn't. I was unhappy, stressed, and constantly thinking about how I could force a better supply. My mental energy was always on breastfeeding. What was I doing right? What was I doing wrong? What else could I do? I was overeating due to the stress. The baby weight wasn't budging.

It wasn't working.

I talked with my husband who helped soothe my mindset further regarding formula feeding. I started to accept the fact that Micah would be okay on formula. Brian reminded me that I had chosen a really good formula, and it didn't make him sick the way it did my daughter.

I needed to let it go. I started to feel better slowly, and it felt good to talk through my lingering fear.

I did feel sad for a few hours as I accepted that he would only be able to get less than one bottle a day of breast milk from me. In the back of my mind, however, I knew I had to feel this way to move forward, to let go and accept my reality as it was. Hey, and maybe my milk would still come in! Or not. But I had released my attachment to it.

He could get one bottle a day from me, and probably one bottle a day from my donor. "That's still better than nothing!" I thought.

In thinking this one positive thought, more positive thoughts started to follow. Micah enjoyed his first three months drinking breast milk almost exclusively. "Wow, that is so great," I realized. "Those first three months of drinking formula are the hardest on the baby's body because their digestive system is less developed, and he got that breast milk. He will be okay now on the formula." Once I turned my attitude toward positivity instead of negativity, it was easier to decide willingly upon constructive thoughts. They felt better than all the negative crap my ego screamed at me!

Unconditional Love

As women, many of us are excellent at putting ourselves and our needs last. I can verify that I do this way more often than I should. I often am running around the house like a chicken with my head cut off. Getting juice, cleaning up after my kids, flipping the laundry, packing lunches, turning a movie on for my daughter, feeding my son, cleaning the kids' rooms... the list can be a million miles long. And yes, all these things need to get done, and I even enjoy doing some of these things, but I get so enveloped in taking care of everyone else that I don't take time for myself. I don't take time to do my hobbies the way I should. For months after my son was born, I wasn't running. I can't remember the last time I scrapbooked. They seem so unimportant compared to caring for my family, or compared to whatever else keeps me busy. But, I forget that I am important too. I need to be taken care of.

Would we tell our daughters (or sons) to not develop their talents and hobbies, or to take care of everyone else before themselves? Or would we tell them to build a deep, loving bond with who they are and what they deserve? Wouldn't we tell them that they deserve the world? They deserve to put themselves first and keep themselves healthy, happy, stress-free, passionate, spiritually fulfilled, forgiving, and kind toward others and themselves. They deserve to live a life of joy, to come alive and do what makes them happy. We would tell them to put any bad feelings aside and let go of thoughts that don't honor them. We would not tell them to put their well-being aside so they can "get more done" the way we do.

As adults, we deserve the same. And, dare I say, if we aren't living a life where we show this much compassion and joy to ourselves and our needs, then we are being poor role models in this area. For whatever reason, life has conditioned this idea of putting ourselves first out of a lot of us. And then it has become a habit, and we have slowly started applying it to more and more areas of life. How is this serving us?

Read the following paragraphs and then close your eyes and envision it. Linger with what it would look like and feel like to be this other person for about a minute or so.

> ### Visualization Exercise
>
> I want you to imagine that you have a clone of yourself. A twin. She is very happy, easygoing, free, and spiritually fulfilled. She has chosen joy in times where you have chosen frustration. She is good at letting things roll off when she is irritated. She loves her family and has found a balance between taking care of her needs, and her family's needs. Her children are growing up with so much love that they are able to meet their own needs and not view it as selfish or negative to do so. She enjoys life, she finds it exciting and invigorating because she decided not to let her struggles lead to negative emotions when she doesn't want them to. She never guilts herself or forces herself into doing anything because she is secure that the universe will give her exactly and everything she needs at the right time.
>
> She has practiced and lives powerfully from the idea that *struggle* doesn't serve her, that the path to clarity *is* the good feeling path, the path of less resistance, and the path of acceptance. She controls her mindset and she feels good when she does. She is completely at ease with who she is and every circumstance going on around her. Not because all areas of her life are perfect, but because she is mentally strong enough to accept and appreciate them anyway.

CHAPTER 4 – A LOVE-CENTERED PERSPECTIVE

What would your breastfeeding journey look like if it came from a place of unconditional love? What would this other woman tell you to do?

It wasn't until I reached my breaking point with trying to force more milk by trying everything I could think of, and was on the brink yet again of stopping breastfeeding altogether out of frustration, that I was finally in a place where I could take a step back and say to myself, "What I'm doing isn't working, and I need to find clarity." Only when I felt like I didn't have any other option could I get to this place, though, and I wish I had been able to let go sooner.

My world started to shift when I viewed my breastfeeding journey through the eyes of unconditional love. Talking with other mom friends and family, I was able to accept that breastfeeding doesn't have to be all or nothing. It doesn't have to be black and white. It doesn't have to be providing a full supply for baby and trying everything to do so, or stopping entirely.

But what does that mean, "Unconditional Love"? To me, it means that I love and respect myself, my happiness and health. It means that this respect is not tied to conditions such as producing a certain amount of milk for my baby (or even producing at all!). My self-worth, my decision making, and my success are not tied to the external conditions of what I can do. My inner feelings are not a product of my conditions in my outer world. I don't need the conditions of my world to change so I can feel good. I can feel good even with those conditions!! My self-worth is separate because I can choose it to be so. I respect myself enough to choose my thoughts deliberately so I am an emotionally well person. I choose to love myself whether I produce 10 ml, 4 oz., or none at all. My value as a mom or person is no longer about what happens in the conditions of my physical world; it's about my mindset of unconditional love toward myself that empowers my emotions.

But, my gosh, as a type A personality this really took a lot of un-conditioning of my thoughts. It took a lot of thought work and time. The next chapter is all about this thought work.

CHAPTER 5

SELF COACHING MODEL

This image from one of my favorite life coaches, Brooke Castillo, represents how thoughts manifest into things in the physical world. Our thoughts can be negative and create a result that we don't like, or they can be positive and create the positive results we want. When we are able to change our thoughts, we are capable of viewing our lives from a place of unconditional love, freedom, joy, and empowerment.

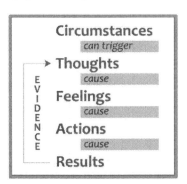

Figure 1. Self Coaching Model. Reprinted from *The Genius of Brooke Castillo's Self Coaching Model*, 2016. Retrieved from: www.wherethelightplays.com/blog/2016/brooke-castillo-self-coaching-model Copyright 2016 by Georgie Bryant.

Brooke Castillo is a renowned life coach and public figure. She created the Self Coaching Model [1] to show us how our thoughts are directly related to our results. We can use the Self Coaching Model to solve our problems and help our mindset shift regarding breastfeeding (or anything else!). Her model connects concepts which are conventional and packages them in a way that serves as a helpful tool which we can use to bring intention and meaning not just into our breastfeeding journeys, but into our lives as a whole. Suzy Rosenstein, another life coach who uses the model, reminds us, "When you use the model, you need to remember this: you are not your thoughts. You are the watcher of your thoughts" [2] (2018). This important distinction provides empowerment and immediate relief for us because it gets us out of the mind space we are stuck in, and into another, more relaxed and distanced zone as an observer.

Let's talk through the model.

Circumstances

When we experience life, events occur throughout our days. We are experiencing circumstances. Circumstances are out of our control; they are facts or events that are happening. Here are some examples of circumstances:

- I arrived late to work today due to traffic.
- My cat peed on the carpet.
- My toddler pooped in her underwear at the park and I have no wipes or new pants to change her into.
- I weigh 215 lbs.
- I stepped in dog poop.
- My husband said, "Isn't next Saturday your birthday?"

These are all situations that are facts in our world. But they are inherently neither good nor bad. They are neutral in and of themselves. It is our decision to apply positivity or negativity to them using our thoughts.

You might argue, "NO WAY!! Your cat peeing on the carpet is annoying! In no way is it good or neutral!" Although that is a common idea that most people would agree with, it's actually a thought that you're having about the circumstance. You may get many people to agree with you, but it doesn't mean that it's true. Your thought is your choice, and it is only as true as you decide it to be from your perception. Your circumstance is the cat peeing, and your thought is that you don't like it. Our circumstances cause thoughts.

Thoughts

Our circumstances cause thoughts, but what thoughts we choose to keep and what thoughts we choose to dismiss are up to us. This is where our power lies. This is where we put ourselves on a spiral of positivity or negativity.

Here are some examples of thoughts:
- *I'm fat.*
- *My shoes smell disgusting.*
- *I'm mad that my daughter won't tell me when she needs to use the potty.*
- *My husband never remembers my birthday.*
- *I need more money to pay my trash bill.*
- *I am struggling to produce enough breast milk for my baby.*

Let's continue with the example that your toddler pooped in her pants at the park and you have no wipes or spare pants. Ha! Your first thought might be something like:

"Oh, man, that is disgusting, what are we gonna do?"

If you continue along the spiral of negativity, you might keep going along with something like this, blaming yourself, or your husband...

"Why didn't you grab the diaper bag?"

"I told you to grab it when we left the house."

"What are we gonna do now?"

"Great, now we have to leave, her brother is gonna be upset, and my car is gonna smell so bad."

"She's never gonna be potty trained!"

The thoughts continue on and on until you decide they stop. In fact, it's worse if you keep going because they start to gain momentum and soon they feel as if they have more power over you than you'd like.

What if, instead, you are aware of your thoughts and you choose to stop them when they start going in a direction that you don't wish? It could go something like this:

"Oh, man, she pooped her pants." (circumstance)

"Do we have any wipes or extra pants? No? Okay."

"What do we have in the trunk that we may be able to use?"

"Okay, we have an old sock we can wipe her with and just throw out, and one of my shirts that I can wrap around her waist."

"It's not perfect but we will make do."

"We might have to leave early, but that's okay. Her little brother will just have to learn the need to care for others..."

Do you see how these are two totally different energies that you end up with? When you change your thoughts to those you prefer, you are opening yourself to not only a different mood, but a different outcome. You're also able to receive new ideas because you are in a positive and receptive mindset. This can change your outcome further. You have the ultimate power: you can choose any thought you'd like. The possibilities are endless.

***

It is a huge problem that, as we go about our day to day lives, we aren't really aware of our thoughts and feelings. Moreover, there are many of us who believe we can't control our feelings at all, and we are at the mercy of whatever feeling washes over us. I can't stress enough that this simply isn't true; we have control over our feelings when we are deliberate and intentional in our thoughts. Our thought patterns create how we will feel about something.

Feelings

Let's continue along the Self Coaching Model. Your thought about the circumstance then creates feelings. You are now changing an idea to a belief. Your shoes stepped in dog poop and you think it's disgusting. Therefore, to you and your perception, it is disgusting. You believe that, and you feel disgusted.

In the example in which we leave the park angry, we develop discord with our spouse (or ourselves), and with a little brother who is upset that he has to leave too. Later in the day it may even spiral out of control and produce more actions and decisions that aren't what we want. Maybe we then burn dinner or skip sex with our spouse because of our attitude. I've personally experienced that quick downward spiral from small initial triggers.

Instead, if we leave the park in a positive mindset, the family is more at peace with each other and the situation. Perhaps we have even used the poopy pants as an example to teach the little brother patience for those who are having a bad day. It is more likely that later in the day we keep our patience and enjoy the evening more fully, whatever it brings, when we intentionally choose thoughts that create the emotions we prefer.

Well-known inspirational speaker and author, Esther Abraham-Hicks, gives us an emotional guidance scale to judge how we are feeling.

The organization of the spiral in the illustration that follows shows us which emotion feels better or worse than others. For example, optimism feels better than revenge. Of course. Okay, here's one more subtle distinction. If you are feeling negative, blame feels better than anger. These feelings gain momentum the longer you focus on them. This is an important concept that we can use to our advantage. First, let's take a look at an example. If you are jealous about your friend winning the lottery, then the more you focus on it, the more jealous you will feel, or perhaps you may even continue down the spiral and start to feel insecure or depressed that you didn't win. This tendency of good thoughts to attract more good thoughts and bad thoughts to attract more bad thoughts is called the Law of Attraction. It will give you more of what you're focusing on. If you choose positive thoughts, you will gain more positive thoughts. If you choose negative ones, you'll gain more negative ones. In her blog, *Living Lovelee*, Leeor Alexandra discusses Abraham-Hicks' concept and notes that all it takes is 17 seconds for your energy to shift, and in 68 seconds more thoughts like it begin to occur and gain momentum [3] (Alexandra, 2017)

CHAPTER 5 – SELF COACHING MODEL

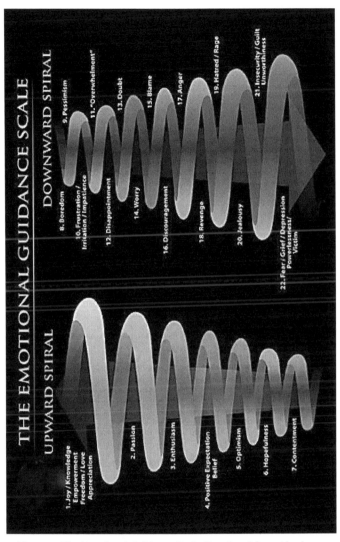

Figure 2. The Emotional Guidance Scale. Reprinted from Abraham-Hicks Emotional Guidance Scale, 2015. Retrieved from: toc-now.com/abraham-hicks-emotional-guidance-scale/ Copyright 2015 by Andrea Schulman

Another thing to note with this graphic is that our best selves, represented by that woman from the meditation, are always living at the top of the spiral. The idea of unconditional love is always paramount, and what our souls truly desire. Therefore, we always feel best when we choose thoughts that lead to feelings of unconditional love, empowerment, joy, appreciation, and freedom. We feel most at peace when we are aligned with these higher, positive emotions.

On the other hand, when our thoughts and our feelings aren't aligned with what our best, loving self would choose, we feel negative emotions. We've been conditioned to believe that negative emotions are inevitable and a fact of life. But what if, just like the sensation of physical pain, negative emotions are a way of warning us we are making the wrong choices? A way of giving us the feedback we need in order to make a different decision before we end up really hurt? Abraham-Hicks argues this is because we are separate from unconditional love (or what she refers to as Source Energy):

> You do, without meaning to, a fairly extensive job of pinching yourself off from who you really are. Anytime you are feeling any negative emotion, no matter how mild or extreme it is, that negative emotion is the indication of the pinching-off-edness. [...] So, when you realize you are an extension of Source Energy, and the better you feel, the more you are allowing the whole of you in the moment [4] (Abraham-Hicks, 2014, 1:10–1:43).

Abraham-Hicks refers to this scale as our inner guidance system. We can use it like a guide our lives, like a GPS, steering us toward the happiness and fulfillment we crave. She writes:

> The navigational system never asks, 'Where have you been?' It does not ask: 'Why have you been there so long?' Its only mission is to assist you in getting from where you are to where you want to be. Your emotions provide a similar guidance system for you, for their primary function is also to help you travel the distance from where you are to wherever you want to be [5] (Hicks & Hicks, 2004, p. 87).

The power behind this quote lies in the idea that we cannot move forward by dwelling in past emotions. It does nothing to help us move forward when we keep our thoughts on the whys or the situations of the past. We don't have to overanalyze to move forward either. We don't need to head back to childhood and dig up a justification as to why we are feeling the way we do. We simply need to work with the emotion we are experiencing now, and if we want to change it, then we find thoughts to change it.

We search for thoughts that allow our best self, the unconditional love for ourselves, to start shining through. The second part of this book will contain tools to help us do exactly that — to find thoughts that serve us and then practice to keep our focus on those positive thoughts. When we are thinking a thought that our best selves would disagree with, we experience that feedback by feeling a negative emotion. On the other hand, when we think thoughts that honor who we are and what we want, we experience positive emotions.

For example, when I had Allie and I struggled with breastfeeding, I felt almost all the negative emotions on the downward spiral: I felt I wasn't good enough, and was mad that I felt like I couldn't do better. I beat myself up, and I felt anger, blame, overwhelm, frustration, disappointment, and even unworthiness when I quit early. Knowing what I know now, my best self was disagreeing with me. She loved me unconditionally, and I was being way too hard on myself. Love is unconditional; that means it doesn't judge when I can't do something. Love doesn't care how much milk I could produce for her or how long I breastfed her. Unconditional love loves us, well, without condition!

Action

These feelings then lead us to action, inaction, or re-action [6] (Castillo, 2019). Many people recognize this connection when the feeling is negative. When we are angry, we sometimes yell. When we are sad, we may overeat. When we are frustrated, we are short with our communication. There are also times when this connection may be trickier to see, but it is still there. When we are feeling jealous, we might make underhanded comments or looks. When we are happy, we make better food choices. When we are feeling hopeful, we may choose more inspiring words when we speak to others. The connection between how we feel and what we do (or don't do) exists. In being aware of that connection we can find the results we want.

Results

What we take action upon then leads to results. This may happen right away, or it may happen gradually over time. These results we want are correlated with our thoughts. In general, a positive result comes from choosing a positive thought, and a negative result comes from a negative thought.

For example, let's say I am feeling unhappy with my weight. If I don't change my thoughts about my self-view, I will struggle instead of having an easier path. If I think, "I'm fat," I probably won't sign up for a 5k. I probably will feel yucky, and will possibly even eat some chocolate to make myself feel better. If I changed my mindset, just a bit, then I could lead myself into different results. If instead, I thought, "I'm overweight but I can change that," I would have a very different vibe in my emotions. I then might try to go for a walk, or might eat fruit instead of chocolate for my dessert one night. This will then attract more thoughts like it as long as I am staying in this positive mindset, and over time this will lead to more success. If I keep thinking positive thoughts, it will turn into a habit, and other healthy habits will follow.

A Few Important Notes

There are a few more important things to note regarding Brooke Castillo's model. Firstly, you cannot control anyone else. We all have free will, and even if we can manipulate some people in certain situations, in general we cannot force someone to behave how we want them to. You may think that you would feel better if you control someone else. "Why won't my baby just sleep the night?! If he would, I'd be so much happier!" No, you choose to pursue the feeling of happiness first because you want to have it, then you brainstorm some positive thoughts you'd like to have about your baby not sleeping that will get you to the positive feeling. The problem will resolve itself, but not by you forcing someone else to change.

Secondly, the thought you choose needs to be believable in order to actually change your emotions. It will not work if you choose a thought that you do not believe. For example, if you want to lose weight, and you choose the thought that you will log your meals and lose 20 pounds in two weeks so you can fit into a cocktail dress, but deep down you know that has never happened for you (the most you've ever lost in two weeks is five pounds), it will not happen. It might be hopeful thinking, but it doesn't really feel true for you. It's more like grasping at success, or trying to force it. You know that it takes more than two weeks to lose 20 pounds. In order to change your emotions, choose a thought you believe to be true. If you don't believe it to be true, it will not happen.

On the following page you'll see a summary of the model.

CHAPTER 5 — SELF COACHING MODEL

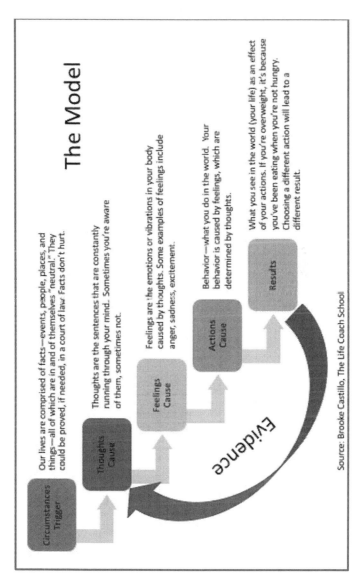

Figure 3. Brooke Castillo's Self Coaching Model Summary. Reprinted from G. Gibbins Coaching LLC, 2019. Retrieved from: www.gerigibbons.com/2016/08/17/solve-any-problem-part1

CHAPTER 6

USING THE SELF COACHING MODEL

Intentionally Choosing Thoughts to Lead to a Specific Emotion

Our feelings are vibrations that lead us to act. It may seem odd to think about feelings as a form of vibration, but it is true. We know we vibrate because we are energy, and all energy vibrates. According to LifeCoachCode.com, "fast vibrations create short-term emotions and more active, conscious reaction. Slow vibrations create long-term emotions and more passive, subconscious reactions"[7] (Davcevski, 2013). Physiologically, our body then reacts to feelings with chemical substances, causing our emotions.

We can empower ourselves to be happy when we realize we can create any feeling we want by finding a thought that will produce the vibration we desire! We can even decide to stop thinking about a subject that is irritating us when we can't find a thought we like about it. We can then dive into the past or the future and find thoughts that do please us to raise our vibrations, and produce an outcome we would like.

For example, let's say you are worried about having enough time (or sanity) to pump X number of times a day. You feel like you just don't want to pump, but you also don't want *not* to pump. You can't seem to talk your way around it to yourself or anyone else. No one can really give you a good solution. You're stuck.

Do you think you'll get a new idea about how to fix the problem when you're stuck in your negative vibe? Probably not, but you'll probably get more thoughts that confuse you. In fact, Law of Attraction says so. The thoughts you choose to have will attract similar thoughts.

The Law of Attraction

If we think of our feelings as vibrational energy, the Law of Attraction is essentially saying that when we focus on a certain vibration (emotion), more of that vibration (emotion) will be attracted to us.[8] To change what we are attracting to ourselves, we need to change the vibrations (emotions) we are creating. If you focus on negatives, you will act upon and see negative results. If you are able to focus on the positives — especially the powerful positives like passion, joy, love, freedom, and enlightenment — then you will receive more of those. This is as much common sense as it is, as some people call it, "a law of the universe."

Now, let's clear something up. I don't believe that you can think about something for a few seconds and, *TA-DA*, it appears. Umm, no. Otherwise we'd all be millionaires. However, the Self Coaching Model lays out for us how circumstances we experience eventually turn into results, but we have control over what those results will be via the thoughts we choose, the feelings we feel as a result, and the actions we take. The Law of Attraction reminds us that when we choose our thoughts, the feelings we then feel will attract similar thoughts and feelings, strengthening and amplifying this cycle. You have the power to create new circumstances for yourself.

This cycle of circumstance > thought > feeling > action > result/circumstance, etc., is constantly taking place whether you are aware of it or not. And the stronger your focus on the emotion, on the feeling you are feeling, the more intensely the Law of Attraction works to bring you similar feelings and experiences. We will use this concept later in a positive way to help us reach whatever goals we set for ourselves.

Anger is a great example of LOA (Law of Attraction), bringing similar feelings because it can be a very intense emotion. It is easy to focus on how angry we are. Once we have the vibration in our body that leads to anger, we focus on it and it quickly grows. I could give a specific example but I don't think it's necessary. Just picture your last argument featuring something you were really upset about, and recall how as the conversation got deeper and deeper, you or the other person were quickly able to find more negative thoughts... which then left you angrier and angrier!

Consider these two concepts to move our mindset forward: 1) LOA says we attract more of what we are focused upon and 2) emotionally it benefits us to allow ourselves to experience unconditional love (or as high up on the spiral of positivity as possible). Often, we are resisting feeling good about a topic for one reason or another. It feels justified because of our emotions, but if it isn't how we want to feel, then we don't need to be stuck there. If breastfeeding is a subject area where you feel stuck, then you will continue to attract more of that stuck feeling. You can instantly change your vibration to a better-feeling emotion by thinking about something else more positive, or happier, and meanwhile allowing some of those negative emotions regarding breastfeeding to have less focus, to be less important. Then, LOA will start to eliminate the strength of your negativity on the breastfeeding topic because you aren't giving it more momentum and power with your focus.

The ultimate purpose of this book is to uplift your emotions and thoughts regarding breastfeeding, but you will not be able to get there if you try to force it to happen. Your well-being, your intent to focus on yourself with unconditional love overall has to come first, and then the thought shifts described later in this book will be much more effective because the timing will allow them to be received from a powerful place.

Luckily, this idea of LOA can work for any emotion we are feeling. It doesn't need to be anger. What if you were having a good day, and then just started to focus on what a great day you were having... and it got better and better!? It happens!

Using This Information to Your Advantage

Once the concepts of the Self Coaching Model and the Law of Attraction are understood, you have great self-empowerment. You can use the model to unravel a problem or plan for the future. Brooke Castillo offers the idea that we jump in at any point on the model using the process description that follows (Castillo, 2019). We can then use our focus of emotion to intensify it.

CHAPTER 6 – USING THE SELF COACHING MODEL

Let's play around with this. Here is her process: on a piece of paper, write CTFAR vertically, like this: [6]

> **C** (Circumstance) –
> **T** (Thought) –
> **F** (Feeling) –
> **A** (Action) –
> **R** (Result) –

Ms. Castillo teaches us that we can start at any point in the model and work forward or backwards. Oftentimes, I don't really know why I am feeling the way I am, but I have a feeling I don't like. That's okay, I can change it. I jump in on the model under F.

> **C** –
> **T** –
> **F** – Sad.
> **A** –
> **R** –

Now I will work my way backward. Why am I feeling sad? What is the thought that led to my sad emotion?

> **C** –
> **T** – I don't think I will be able to go part-time at my job to be a stay-at-home mommy.
> **F** – Sad.
> **A** –
> **R** –

You could keep going with the whole model, or stop there. It might simply be enough to *be aware* of the feeling and why, and decide to change it. You may already know you won't get a result you want by thinking that thought and feeling what follows from that thought. If you'd like to continue, you could fill in the rest of the pieces as they make sense to you one by one.

Here is my example of a full model:

> **C** - My husband is afraid of me going part-time at my job. He doesn't think it can happen, considering we desire a larger home
> **T** - I don't think I will be able to go part-time at my job to be a stay-at-home mommy.
> **F** - Sad.
> **A** - Stop looking for part-time positions, continue making decisions with my current salary.
> **R** - I work full-time.

The power lies in your thoughts, because thoughts are essentially decisions. We can control those, and they are at the top of the model — which means they affect everything underneath them. We can also use the model to plan ahead for results or emotions. Castillo (2019) says, "Once you start to use the model, you'll begin to see that you have the power within you to choose what results you want to create. That is power. That is how you change your entire life to be exactly what you want it to be." [6]

For example, I know something is going to happen (circumstance) and I want to control how I react, or how I feel about it.

CHAPTER 6 — USING THE SELF COACHING MODEL

> **C** – I have a low milk supply right now.
> **T** – (I choose my thought to be loving!) **Anything fresh I can feed my baby is better than nothing.**
> **F** – I feel good about what I give my baby because whatever I can provide from me is enough.
> **A** – I continue breastfeeding.
> **R** – Baby is breastfed for as long as I desire!

Remember two things: firstly, a thought you choose is your decision; if you want it to be positive, great! If you are feeling bitter and resentful about something and you want to stay that way, then fine! Keep thinking thoughts that put you where you want to be, and the Law of Attraction will follow with more like it. Secondly, your thought you choose needs to be believable. In this example, I shouldn't have a thought like, "Oh well, my milk is low today, but tomorrow maybe it will double if I drink a lactation shake." I know this isn't true for me, since I have tried it. And because it isn't true, it won't help me feel better. The thought is not believable and therefore does not change my feelings. Let's work on finding some thoughts that are believable and radiate unconditional love.

CHAPTER 7

A THOUGHT FRAMEWORK FOR BREASTFEEDING ISSUES

My Mindset Shift

When I finally felt like it wasn't worth it to breastfeed anymore, I felt sad. I essentially wanted relief, and I felt like this was the only way to get it. Quitting meant I could stop pumping, stop stressing and stop taking up so much space in my mind about it. My milk was about three to four ounces a day total, which wasn't even enough for one bottle for my baby. At four months into my journey, it wasn't feeling worth it to continue to pump three times at work and one time (or more) at home to keep my milk at maximum output. It was evident that my milk supply was not going to increase because I had tried all the approaches.

I also felt stressed and was overeating. The baby weight isn't budging; in fact, I was gaining. I gave myself permission to stop overeating and to start cutting my calories down so I could start to lose some of the baby weight. I feared that it would affect my milk, and it did. Eating less cut my milk down to less than two ounces a day initially and even more later on, but being overweight was a significant aspect of my life that needed to be changed.

It was time for a new perspective. Was I going to quit? Or keep going? What did I really want? What honored me? What would make me feel good? Could I compromise and still be happy with myself? This was an extremely difficult idea for my type A personality. I am a very all-or-nothing person. When I go for something, I go hard, or I stop because it isn't for me. Allowing myself to be in between, in the gray area, would be an uncomfortable new concept for me. I didn't think I would even like it.

I actually started by Googling the all-or-nothing mindset. I did this primarily because I felt like I would be a failure if I didn't think this way. After all, it has helped me achieve some incredible things in my life. I didn't want to let the mindset go. It would be super uncomfortable and I assumed it wouldn't work because it seemed like it was all I knew. I felt like I would think myself to be a slacker. (Ugh, why do I judge myself like this?)

Surprisingly, the websites I read started to convince me that getting away from the all-or-nothing mindset leads to more success than having it. Of course, every instance is different, but one of them gave me an example that I loved.

It said something along the lines of: if you don't have time to do your 30-minute workout and you only have time for eight minutes, then do eight. This is a powerful example because it's pretty uncommon to want to do an eight-minute workout. But it showed that the gray area was more profitable than the all-or-nothing mindset because it calculated how much more exercise time you would have at the end of the year if even twice a week

CHAPTER 7 – A THOUGHT FRAMEWORK FOR BREASTFEEDING ISSUES

you had done an eight minute workout when you wanted to skip. Just 16 minutes a week times 52 weeks = 832 minutes of exercise a year that you otherwise wouldn't have done. Do you think that could make an impact? YES!!!

I began feeling more open-minded and willing to imagine what it might look like for my breastfeeding situation. I remembered my thought work and Brooke Castillo's Self Coaching Model. Was I actually willing to compromise? Would it be worth it?

I decided it was worth it to compromise and give my baby my one ounce a day rather than quit entirely. I felt empowered that I'd be able to say that I stuck with breastfeeding longer, and no matter what my production was, he got fresh breast milk. I decided I would just keep my breastfeeding very low-maintenance instead of stopping. Low maintenance to me would mean I wouldn't be stressing about it at all anymore. I liked that. I was willing to find ways for relief and not give up on my breastfeeding. I used the model to help myself find thought patterns which would lead me to happiness, and then spring me into actions that were appropriate.

My decision was to stop pumping most of the day because it was something that was really robbing me of time. It was ransacking my lunch break at work; I was waking up early to pump (since baby often didn't feed due to sore teeth), and in general I just hated being hooked to a pump. My decision was to pump once a day, whenever that felt right, and to feed on demand as much as my son wanted. It was a decision I could live with, and after a few days of doing it I felt peaceful.

Your Turn

In my opinion, the best thing I can do for you is to help you find an arrangement that works for you that keeps you breastfeeding. If you truly are looking to stop, and not just to find relief and sanity, then go ahead and stop. Check out the chapter on doing so. If you only want to stop out of frustration, then why not work with your thoughts to alleviate that frustration first, before you make a decision to stop pumping or not?

Do you think you might be ready to explore the Self Coaching Model and try it on your own? Let's look at some common breastfeeding issues and pin down thought changes. The idea here is to examine and address our thoughts so they keep our emotions feeling how we want to feel, not simply reacting during what is a very stressful time for most of us!! We will be working with the (T) Thoughts and the (F) Feelings to keep ourselves from the (A) Action of quitting breastfeeding since it is not the (R) Result we want. (Although, if you truly feel that it is right for you, then that is okay too!) Most of these are thoughts I have had! Remember, a quality IBCLC can offer specific advice! These are thoughts to get you started.

Choose a topic from the list below which holds a thought that is similar to yours now. Then, you can go to the corresponding chart(s) where you will see a green AFTER column to offer you some believable thought shifts. You should work on finding your own thought change which feels loving, but these should get you started. You are beginning your thought work! Our next chapter will be about sustaining these new thoughts and goals.

CHAPTER 7 – A THOUGHT FRAMEWORK FOR BREASTFEEDING ISSUES

	TOPICS	
1	I don't make a full supply of breast milk (inadequate milk production). I don't even make half of my baby's needs, so what's the point?	Pg. 54
2	Pumping takes up a lot of time/ I hate pumping.	Pg. 56
3	I can't get baby to latch.	Pg. 59
4	I hate the idea of supplementing or using formula.	Pg. 60
5	I don't have time to breastfeed.	Pg. 62
6	Herbs, prescriptions, and other supplements.	Pg. 63
7	Mastitis/sore nipples and other pains.	Pg. 64
8	Overwhelmed, sick of trying, sick of forcing it.	Pg. 65
9	Guilt over having a breast reduction.	Pg. 67

Topic 1 – Not Enough Milk

BEFORE

T - It's not worth breastfeeding because I don't make a full supply for baby.

F - Boredom, pessimism, frustration, irritation, impatience, overwhelm, doubt, worry, discouragement, anger, revenge, hatred, jealousy, inscuity, guilt, unworthiness, fear, grief, depression, powerlessness.

AFTER

T - I don't need to make a full supply to be successful.

T - I can define what success means; exclusively breastfeeding isn't the only way.

T - I can breastfeed my baby whatever I make and decide that's enough.

T - I am good enough as a mom no matter what I can provide.

T - Baby receives so many benefits from any amount of fresh milk, and I can manage my time for my sanity.

T - I'm willing to try to find a way to continue even if I cannot produce a full supply.

T - My dream is not over because I didn't produce enough milk. A new goal is born and I can find it!

T - I can use the Self Coaching Model to help me handle any emotions that arise due to my decision.

F - Joy, knowledge, empowerment, freedom, love, appreciation, passion, enthusiasm, positive expectation, belief, optimism, hopefulness, and contentment.

CHAPTER 7 – A THOUGHT FRAMEWORK FOR BREASTFEEDING ISSUES

BEFORE

T - It's not worth breastfeeding because I don't make even *half* a supply for baby.

F - Boredom, pessimism, frustration, irritation, impatience, overwhelm, doubt, worry, discouragement, anger, revenge, hatred, jealousy, inscuity, guilt, unworthiness, fear, grief, depression, powerlessness.

AFTER

T - I don't need to make any certain number of ounces to successfully breastfeed.

T - I can choose not to let the amount of my supply be important.

T - I can define what success means; providing more milk than formula isn't the only way.

T - I can breastfeed my baby whatever I make and decide that's enough.

T - I am good enough as a mom no matter what I can provide.

T - Even one teaspoon of breast milk contains thousands to millions of germ-fighting cells; I can make one teaspoon!

T - Maybe I can try an SNS® or Lact-Aid® to keep baby at the breast.

T - I don't have to make a certain amount to make it "worth it", my baby is always worth it.

T - I can breastfeed in a way that isn't stressful and make it for a whole year (or however long I choose).

T - I can use the Self Coaching Model to help me handle any emotions that arise due to my decision.

F - Joy, knowledge, empowerment, freedom, love, appreciation, passion, enthusiasm, positive expectation, belief, optimism, hopefulness, and contentment.

Topic 2 – Pumping Is a Nightmare

BEFORE

T - I don't have time to pump.

F - Boredom, pessimism, frustration, irritation, impatience, overwhelm, doubt, worry, discouragement, anger, revenge, hatred, jealousy, inscuity, guilt, unworthiness, fear, grief, depression, powerlessness.

AFTER

T - Maybe if I make a schedule I will find more time to pump.

T - Perhaps I would feel better about my pumping if I skipped one pump each day.

T - I can find the time to pump.

T - Thinking about not having time to pump is a problem. It's my thoughts that I need to change.

T - I can try to find time in new ways.

T - It's okay if I don't want to find the time to pump as much as I first thought I should. I can still make breastfeeding work.

T - There's no right or wrong amount of times per day to pump.

T - I can use the Self Coaching Model to help me handle any emotions that arise due to my decision.

F - Joy, knowledge, empowerment, freedom, love, appreciation, passion, enthusiasm, positive expectation, belief, optimism, hopefulness, and contentment.

CHAPTER 7 — A THOUGHT FRAMEWORK FOR BREASTFEEDING ISSUES

BEFORE

T - I don't want to pump anymore — I hate it.

F - Boredom, pessimism, frustration, irritation, impatience, overwhelm, doubt, worry, discouragement, anger, revenge, hatred, jealousy, inscuity, guilt, unworthiness, fear, grief, depression, powerlessness.

AFTER

T - I hate pumping because I have chosen that as my thought. I can change that.

T - If I reduce the number of times per day I pump, I may not hate it as much.

T - Maybe I should write down why I think I hate it and look with a rational mind.

T - No one is forcing me to pump. I don't have to pump. I can simply do my best to feed my child when he / she will take the breast.

T - Maybe I can pump when I feel like it and breastfeed the rest of the time.

T - When worries come up about my supply dropping due to less time pumping, I can use my Self Coaching Model to address them.

T - I can use the Self Coaching Model to help me handle any emotions that arise due to my decision.

F - Joy, knowledge, empowerment, freedom, love, appreciation, passion, enthusiasm, positive expectation, belief, optimism, hopefulness, and contentment.

BEFORE

T - It hurts to pump and I want to stop.

F - Boredom, pessimism, frustration, irritation, impatience, overwhelm, doubt, worry, discouragement, anger, revenge, hatred, jealousy, inscuity, guilt, unworthiness, fear, grief, depression, powerlessness.

AFTER

T - Although I am currently experiencing discomfort, I can find ways to alleviate it.

T - This discomfort could get better with time (if I am at the beginning of my breastfeeding journey).

T - I could probably do a Google search or talk to other moms and find ways to make this more bearable.

T - Maybe I could use a manual pump instead of an electric.

T - Perhaps I can find relief with an IBCLC or with information from a doctor. My insurance may cover this. Even just a phone call!

T - If I cannot find pain relief, it is okay to pump at a lower intensity or stop pumping all together. It's more important that my mental health and wellbeing come first so I can be strong for my baby.

T - I can use the Self Coaching Model to help me handle any emotions that arise due to my decision.

F - Joy, knowledge, empowerment, freedom, love, appreciation, passion, enthusiasm, positive expectation, belief, optimism, hopefulness, and contentment.

CHAPTER 7 – A THOUGHT FRAMEWORK FOR BREASTFEEDING ISSUES

Topic 3 – I Can't Get Baby to Latch

BEFORE

T - I am frustrated (or scared, etc.) that baby won't latch.

F - Boredom, pessimism, frustration, irritation, impatience, overwhelm, doubt, worry, discouragement, anger, revenge, hatred, jealousy, inscuity, guilt, unworthiness, fear, grief, depression, powerlessness.

AFTER

T - I forgive myself for not being able to get this right away.
T - It's okay to supplement until I get this.
T - Undue pressure on myself will not help the situation.
T - I choose to stay positive about this.
T - I can get help getting baby to latch. I can ask moms online in a group or use an IBCLC for help.
T - I choose patience with myself and my baby.
T - I can do this. I can find ways to make this work.
T - My baby and I will be grateful I persevered through this challenge.
T - Once I have tried everything possible, I give myself permission to stop when it no longer feels honoring to me.
T - I can use the Self Coaching Model to help me handle any emotions that arise due to my decisions.

F - Joy, knowledge, empowerment, freedom, love, appreciation, passion, enthusiasm, positive expectation, belief, optimism, hopefulness, and contentment.

Topic 4 – Supplementing with Formula

BEFORE

T - I really don't want to use formula.

F - Boredom, pessimism, frustration, irritation, impatience, overwhelm, doubt, worry, discouragement, anger, revenge, hatred, jealousy, inscuity, guilt, unworthiness, fear, grief, depression, powerlessness.

AFTER

T - It's okay to have that preference but I don't need to let it rule how I feel about feeding my child.
T - Formula is there as a tool to help us.
T - Without formula, many babies would die.
T - Formula will feed my baby appropriately and that really is what matters most.
T - Formulas are becoming more advanced and are much more similar to breast milk than ever before.
T - Many babies are raised exclusively on formula and they are smart, beautiful, and healthy.
T - Some moms who aren't struggling don't want to breastfeed and go straight to formula.
T - There's no shame in using formula except the shame I choose to assign to it.
T - Formula saves babies who have trouble latching or are premature and unable to eat from the breast.
T - I bet I could find donor milk so I can use less.
T - I can use the Self Coaching Model to help me handle any emotions that arise due to my decisions.

F - Joy, knowledge, empowerment, freedom, love, appreciation, passion, enthusiasm, positive expectation, belief, optimism, hopefulness, and contentment.

CHAPTER 7 – A THOUGHT FRAMEWORK FOR BREASTFEEDING ISSUES

BEFORE

T - Formula is making / will make my baby sick.

F - Boredom, pessimism, frustration, irritation, impatience, overwhelm, doubt, worry, discouragement, anger, revenge, hatred, jealousy, inscuity, guilt, unworthiness, fear, grief, depression, powerlessness.

AFTER

T - I can work with the doctor to find formulas that will make baby less sick or not sick at all.

T - Formulas are advancing at a rapid rate with scientific breakthroughs. They are structurally more like breast milk than ever before.

T - It could be something else making my baby sick. I might want to re-examine the whole picture with a professional.

T - Maybe I could try other things to help control any belly issues – pre/probiotics, gas drops, etc.

T - I bet I could find donor milk so I can use less.

T - I can use the Self Coaching Model to help me handle any emotions that arise due to my decisions.

F - Joy, knowledge, empowerment, freedom, love, appreciation, passion, enthusiasm, positive expectation, belief, optimism, hopefulness, and contentment.

Topic 5 – I Don't Have Time to Breastfeed

BEFORE

T - I don't have time to breastfeed, so what's the point?

F - Boredom, pessimism, frustration, irritation, impatience, overwhelm, doubt, worry, discouragement, anger, revenge, hatred, jealousy, inscuity, guilt, unworthiness, fear, grief, depression, powerlessness.

AFTER

T - I need to examine if this is really true.
T - What times am I finding it difficult to breastfeed? How might I be able to plan for this?
T - Is it important that I breastfeed?
T - Do I make time for other important things in my life? How?
T - What times of day / night can I realistically breastfeed?
T - When baby refuses the breast, am I willing to pump instead to keep a supply going?
T - What barriers are getting in the way? How can I creatively resolve them?
T - I can get something to entertain my older child while I breastfeed, or involve them in the process.
T - If baby takes too long at the breast, maybe I can just put her on there for as long as I can.
T - If baby takes too long at the breast and I supplement, maybe I can use an SNS® or Lact-Aid® to shorten the length of time.
T - Perhaps I can just breastfeed when I do have the time.
T - I can use the Self Coaching Model to help me handle any emotions that arise due to my decisions.

F - Joy, knowledge, empowerment, freedom, love, appreciation, passion, enthusiasm, positive expectation, belief, optimism, hopefulness, and contentment.

Topic 6 – Supplements, Herbs, Prescriptions

BEFORE

T - Herbs and prescriptions are not working for me (circumstance). I'm sick of trying with them (F).

F - Boredom, pessimism, frustration, irritation, impatience, overwhelm, doubt, worry, discouragement, anger, revenge, hatred, jealousy, insecurity, guilt, unworthiness, fear, grief, depression, powerlessness.

AFTER

T - I need to examine if this is really true. Am I taking them correctly and consistently?

T - Have I given the herbs / prescriptions a long enough chance to work?

T - Is it critical that I take them? Is there a consequence if I don't?

T - Are there new herbs that I haven't tried that may work?

T - Am I expecting herbs to give me a full supply if, perhaps, that isn't possible? Could I just appreciate any help they do give me?

T - It's okay not to use herbs or prescriptions for any reason I deem necessary.

T - Whatever I can provide, I can choose for it to be enough.

T - Even one teaspoon of breastmilk each day is worth it.

T - I can use the Self Coaching Model to help me handle any emotions that arise due to my decisions.

F - Joy, knowledge, empowerment, freedom, love, appreciation, passion, enthusiasm, positive expectation, belief, optimism, hopefulness, and contentment.

Topic 7 – Mastitis, Sore Nipples, and Other Breast-Related Pains

BEFORE

T - Actually, here the feeling of pain is causing the problem. But pain can cause thoughts that don't honor us.

Let's work on changing the pain and thoughts together.

F - Boredom, pessimism, frustration, irritation, impatience, overwhelm, doubt, worry, discouragement, anger, revenge, hatred, jealousy, inscuity, guilt, unworthiness, fear, grief, depression, powerlessness.

AFTER

T - What are some appropriate ways I can get help with pain management?

T - What have I tried that has helped a little in the past?

T - It is possible to be in pain and be hopeful at the same time.

T - I can research or see a professional to identify the source of pain correctly. That will put me one step forward toward fixing it.

T - I can be less emotional about my pain. I can treat it like any other illness and fix it.

T - I don't have to stop due to the pain if I don't want to stop.

T - If I keep focusing on my end result of what I want my breastfeeding journey to look like, I will get there.

T - A lactation consultant can help me with this.

T - I can find one that I can afford, even if it's just over the phone.

T - Other experienced moms could help me. I could maybe find a group.

T - Is there a vitamin or supplement I could take? Am I taking them correctly and consistently?

F - Joy, knowledge, empowerment, freedom, love, appreciation, passion, enthusiasm, positive expectation, belief, optimism, hopefulness, and contentment.

Topic 8 – Feeling Overwhelmed with Forcing It, etc.

This one starts with a feeling. Write out your Self Coaching Model.

```
C –
T – ???
F – Overwhelmed, sick of trying, sick of forcing it.
A –
R –
```

What thought is causing you to feel overwhelmed and sick of trying? Take a deep breath and calm yourself. Identify it. You can find it. (It may be one listed under the topics.) Now, can you work through it? How is that thought serving you? What emotion would you prefer to have? What thought would lead there? Are you willing to let go of your current emotion so you can feel your new one? Are you willing to let go of an unrealistic expectation you may have been holding yourself to?

Also, if you are sick of trying, sick of forcing it, I personally really encourage you to find a way to step back from your physical reality, and reconnect with your spiritual truths. We are all spiritual beings who have come from a greater place of love when we were born. We were 100 percent connected to this love before we were physical beings, and are still connected to this love as physical beings.

A huge problem for most of us is that we are "doers" and want to manipulate our physical reality so it makes us happy. We are happy by nature. It is our thoughts that have gone against that unconditional love that make us unhappy.

Find your path to happiness *first,* and the Law of Attraction will bring you more of what you're feeling! Use the Self Coaching Model and the next chapter to help you identify thoughts which trigger emotions of happiness and keep them coming!

CHAPTER 7 — A THOUGHT FRAMEWORK FOR BREASTFEEDING ISSUES

Topic 9 – Guilt Over Having a Breast Reduction

BEFORE

T - Actually, here the feeling of guilt / regret is causing the problem. We are working with (F).

Try a CTFAR chart to identify why you feel guilt or regret over the breast reduction. Here are some new thoughts which may help replace old ones.

F - Boredom, pessimism, frustration, irritation, impatience, overwhelm, doubt, worry, discouragement, anger, revenge, hatred, jealousy, inscuity, guilt, unworthiness, fear, grief, depression, powerlessness.

AFTER

T - When I decided to have the reduction, I was not fully aware of how much impact it would have: physically, emotionally, etc.

T - I made the best decision I could at the time.

T - I have enjoyed many of the other benefits that my surgery has brought me. They were / still are important.

T - My decision to feel guilt or regret is my choice. I can choose a better thought and feeling.

T - Regret or guilt are not useful emotions for the happy life I deserve.

T - I choose to let go of negative emotion.

T - I am deserving of happiness.

T - Thinking about do-overs is unhelpful.

T - I can imagine my best breastfeeding journey as am I now, post-surgery.

T - I choose to remember that it is unhelpful to focus on what-if's.

F - Joy, knowledge, empowerment, freedom, love, appreciation, passion, enthusiasm, positive expectation, belief, optimism, hopefulness, and contentment.

CHAPTER 8

SUSTAINING NEW THOUGHTS AND GOALS

We have suitably identified feelings and thoughts that are not working for us. (Remember, this can be done at any time, and often needs to be done over and over.) Now that we have identified how we don't want to feel, we have created a new desire about how we do want to feel.

We have also begun to do the work. Our work is not physical action so much at first, as much as it is thought work. This is an integral switch. Work smarter, not harder. We will feel most in control and most empowered when we keep our thoughts monitored and positive, because we know it will produce a feeling, and eventually an outcome we can agree with.

"How can I stay motivated to be on top of my thoughts when I have a newborn, a toddler, I am exhausted and I have no time?" you ask. Well, just like anything else, you need to decide who is going to be in control of your life. There are a million times a day that we can clear up space in our heads. We are constantly looking for a break. In fact, I dare say that many of us escape to the digital world of Facebook, Instagram, Snapchat, or other social media quite often throughout the day. What if you decided to use just some of that time to be mindful of how you were feeling instead? To be mindful of your thoughts and opinions about the events of the day. Wouldn't this be a more productive use of your time? I can tell you that when I practice this regularly, I actually feel much more rested when I focus on my thoughts rather than everyone else's social-media-curated day.

Although it can be overwhelming, can you focus on just one thought for the upcoming day that puts you on your path? Which one can it be? How do you plan to help yourself sustain it if you start to hear a little voice talking you out of it?

Let me tell you an old Cherokee story called "The Tale of Two Wolves," taken from the Nanticoke Indian Tribe: [9]

> One evening, an elderly Cherokee brave told his grandson about a battle that goes on inside people.
>
> He said, "My son, the battle is between two 'wolves' inside us all. One is evil. It is anger, envy, jealousy, sorrow, regret, greed, arrogance, self-pity, guilt, resentment, inferiority, lies, false pride, superiority, and ego.
>
> "The other is good. It is joy, peace, love, hope, serenity, humility, kindness, benevolence, empathy, generosity, truth, compassion, and faith."
>
> The grandson thought about it for a minute and then asked his grandfather: "Which wolf wins?"
>
> The old Cherokee simply replied, "The one you feed."

CHAPTER 8 — SUSTAINING NEW THOUGHTS AND GOALS

Where we turn our attention is the winning factor. And, it's all about practice. The longer you choose to feed your "good wolf" by choosing empowering thoughts, the stronger the habit becomes, the easier it is to sustain. With each decision to examine your thoughts throughout the day you are mindfully choosing to help yourself (and the good wolf) to win out.

The Focus Wheel

Are you a worrier? If you are like me, you have a recording playing in your mind that never seems to shut off. It is discouraging and unhelpful, to say the least. "What about this?" and "What about that?" our mind thinks. Or even worse, we decide that something will be negative before it even begins. "This can't possibly happen," or "There's not enough time for this." All these thoughts swirling around in our head combined with our focus upon them creates a reality. They are resistance, they are our prior thought patterns thwarting us from allowing ourselves to be in the here and now. They are resistance to allowing unconditional love to find the best path.

Choosing appropriate thoughts gives direction to our empowerment, and using our focus provides intensity, which boosts us toward reaching our goals. We know how to worry... but in a positive way? Is there such a thing? A potent exercise to help us have more intensity in our focus is Abraham-Hicks' focus wheel. In the center of the wheel you're going to write a goal you want to achieve or an outcome you desire. Then, in each of the twelve surrounding sections, you will write related emotions that will grow your positive vibrations. It's mealtime for the good wolf! The following is an image of what it looks like, and then the process described in more detail.

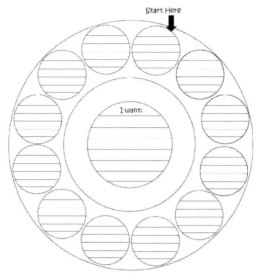

Figure 4. Focus Wheel. Reprinted from *The Focus Wheel Process*, 2012. Retrieved from www.thevortex.me/the-focus-wheel-process/
Copyright 2012 by Merav Knafo

I recommend fully listening to this session[10] that Abraham-Hicks shares with a client, but I will highlight the most important aspects as well from the video below for those of us who are not able to listen right now.

> "A focus wheel will help you to focus. And, its purpose is to help you focus in a more positive direction." (Abraham-Hicks, 2014, 1:26–1:34)
>
> "The focus wheel causes you, right here, right now, to change your vibrational point of attraction." (2:21–2:26)
>
> "In the center of the focus wheel, you make your statement of intent." (2:48–2:52)

> "So now, the focus wheel process begins. If you can envision one of those merry-go-rounds on the playground, and you want to get on, your friends are already on, and they've got it going really fast… you want to get on, you try to get on while it's moving really fast, and you can't. It will just knock you off in the bushes. But if they will slow it down enough so you can get on, then you can speed it up together. And that's what this focus wheel is like. It lets you get on, and then once you're on, you can speed it up a bit. So, the goal is to make a statement you already believe, that matches your desire […] but soft enough that it doesn't challenge your own belief." (3:28-4:13)
>
> "So you just find something that already matches. A belief that you already hold." (4:14-4:18)

In the video, Abraham-Hicks helps her client find a statement that is powerful, true and matches what is in the center of the wheel. Her client then writes that statement in a section of the wheel.

Next, Abraham-Hicks encourages her to make another statement and continue writing. She continues encouraging her to find more and more statements to continue filling each of the 12 pieces.

Step by step, you should:

(1) Download or draw the wheel. You can download and print this PDF from: www.thevortex.me/wp-content/uploads/2012/12/focuswheel.pdf

(2) Identify what you don't want. (Example: I don't want to worry about how much milk I produce.)

(3) From there, create a positive statement about how you want to feel (example: I feel relaxed and satisfied with my breastfeeding) and write the statement in the middle of the wheel.

Here are some examples that I might put in my 12 sections of my wheel:
- I am proud of all the effort I have given it so far.
- My husband tells me I am doing a good job.
- I'm finding support to help me.
- I'm doing good things for my baby no matter how much milk I give him.
- I define what success is.
- My path does not need to be all or nothing.

(4) Continue finding thoughts and feelings that match the center idea. Momentum builds with each section. With each new positive, believable thought you find and affirm in writing, you will feel better and better. Allow yourself to feel overwhelmed yet relaxed by the upper emotions from the guidance scale that wash over you. Don't judge it too much.

As Abraham-Hicks explains, "And now you've romped around with this. Now you want to confirm the statement that is in the middle of your focus wheel, and what that statement is, is I am good at this, I am really good at this, I love how good I am at this! And now your focus wheel has focused you into alignment with who you are — who you are, relative to this point of attraction. Doesn't that feel good?" (Abraham-Hicks, 2014, 8:28–8:46)

(5) When you have completed writing the wheel, re-read all your statements. Notice how much closer you feel to the emotion you desire. Why not re-read them daily?

CHAPTER 8 – SUSTAINING NEW THOUGHTS AND GOALS

Before you get out of bed in the morning (before your brain starts trucking down old paths) is a great time to center yourself and your mindset for the day. Or, right before you go to bed helps set you intention for the close of your day and for your subconscious overnight. It is what we do *habitually* where we will find success. Feed your good wolf *daily*.

(6) Remember, you can write a new wheel any time you want and do this for any subject you wish to feel better about.

Here is an example of a wheel (not breastfeeding related) to help you:

Figure 5. The Focus Wheel Process. Reprinted from *The Focus Wheel: How To Get To The Heart Of Your Heart's Desires*, 2017.
Retrieved from: blog.mindvalley.com/focus-wheel-desires/
Copyright 2017 by Annamaria Nagy

If you need more examples, try watching the videos located in the link below the image.

CHAPTER 9

ENDING THE ADVENTURE

Firstly, let me remind you that there is no one best way to feed your baby. You do not need to breastfeed your child for any reason if you don't want to. If it doesn't feel right, then no one needs you to feel guilty about not wanting to do it. There are hundreds of reasons why women either don't breastfeed, or stop breastfeeding. It's common to stop at six months, 12 months, or even 18 months (no matter if you are experiencing a problem or not). It doesn't matter if you stop at two weeks, two months, or two years. Your problem isn't stopping breastfeeding. Your problem is your thoughts about stopping breastfeeding.

If you have other people in your life who you feel are forcing you to do this and you have little interest, perhaps you should kindly give yourself permission to allow them to take up less of your thoughts. If that person is you, then maybe you really need to tell that voice to be quiet.

Breast milk is certainly a precious gift, but it is only one way out of a million that we can love and bond with our babies. Is it really honoring for you to beat yourself up about this one way to provide for your baby when there are so many more? No, it isn't. Remember, the idea of this book is to help you view yourself from a lens of unconditional love. It is then, and only then, when we are accepting of ourselves, that we can move forward happily and appropriately.

After multiple rounds of thought work, when I considered what might be the appropriate time to stop breast feeding, I realized it would probably be before he is one year old. One personal reason I felt this way is because my baby has lost interest in the breast most days, so I was simply pumping. I don't mind the arrangement terribly, since I didn't pump much at all the last month before my decision. It wasn't stressful and I know our time together has been great. It's the opposite of how my time with Allie was. It's funny: the physical and emotional closeness that I searched for (by having him at the breast) is something I have started to find in other ways. We have times every night where all he wants to do is just lay on me and snuggle me. Ah, it's the best! And it's the same closeness and endorphin rush I felt at the beginning of my breastfeeding journey!

Are you feeling guilty because deep down it is something you want to do but can't seem to find a way to breastfeed without going crazy? Are you still feeling frustrated? I encourage you to check out the thought patterns in the previous chapter first before deciding to quit, and/or contact me!

Okay, let's get back to the idea of our breastfeeding journey coming to an end. I want us to feel at peace when we say to ourselves and others that our time is over. Is it okay to be a tiny bit sad and maybe even a little nostalgic that it is over? Of course it is! You choose your thoughts and the emotions they bring with them, and from what I hear, those are thoughts and emotions that many moms have when they start to wean.

CHAPTER 9 — ENDING THE ADVENTURE

At the time right before my decision, I could feel it would be soon. I knew that when I ended my breastfeeding, I might be a bit sad, but I will have had an overall feeling of joy, love, and fulfillment. I would know that I did the thought work which allowed me to breastfeed from a place of satisfaction and happiness, no longer viewing it as a mountain to climb. I would know that I didn't quit out of frustration, irritation, feeling inadequate, or any type of sadness or regret. I know I will stop breastfeeding while having felt good about everything I provided for my baby. We all deserve to view our journey through this lens of love.

After all, why else did you agree to bring this tiny newborn into this world and give him/her so much of your body, mind, and spirit? Love. Love is always the answer, and love will be involved in how I answer to myself and others when my journey ends. I chose thoughts which lead to emotions that ended my journey through that warm-hearted light.

Here are some positive thoughts I started thinking when I decided it was almost time to stop. I wrote these before I weaned Micah, and I feel happy when I read or speak them now. They resonate with me. It is my wish that you will feel at peace with similar thoughts when the time has come for you:

- I am very proud of myself for breastfeeding for the length of time I did.
- I am so honored to have served my little man in this way.
- I know I am enough: I did enough, I am good enough, and our journey has been enough.
- I feel blessed I could provide any amount that I did, whether it was my maximum number of ounces or a minimum.

- Breastfeeding taught me patience in a way I wasn't sure I could learn it.
- Breastfeeding has helped me be more spiritual and less of a do-er, less of a "forcer" and more of a "grateful allower" of my glorious life experience.
- I am grateful for the bond I built with my baby.
- I have learned more unconditional love for myself throughout this process.
- I feel redeemed for having given up out of frustration with Allison. (Note: I did not need to actually breastfeed this time to let that go... I should have released that much earlier!)
- I am excited by how much I have learned about this topic and I can't wait to share it with others one day.
- It was valuable to experience all the trials and tribulations of pumping and herbs and low supply because it made me feel alive, like a real breastfeeding mom, and as if I were on my path.
- Even though I had a breast reduction, in the end, I could still breastfeed my baby.
- This journey has connected me to many other loving souls who have encouraged and loved me along my path. It was a joy to find these other kind women.
- Success was not defined by the amount I could produce. I made my own definition.
- I can't wait to donate or throw out all my pumping stuff, nursing bras, SNSs, etc.!
- I did it. I actually did it. I breastfed my son.
- I love myself for taking on a new adventure and finding success.
- I'm AWESOME!

CHAPTER 10

MY DESIRES CAME TRUE

When Micah was seven months old, I decided it was time for me to stop. It's funny, because when I became pregnant with him and thought ahead about what I wanted, I thought my desire would be to produce a full supply for my baby. I thought it was what would bring me happiness and closure. I thought it would redeem me for giving up "too early" with Allie. Would an overabundance of supply make me happy? Of course. But why was this so? This was a more important question for me.

When I sat down and thought about my deeper reasons for trying to breastfeed exclusively, I realized that I had already gotten everything I had wanted. My desires had been fulfilled, even without having a full supply.

I had desired:

- A very different experience from my first baby
- To know what it was like to make that huge time sacrifice and be the exclusive feeder
- To connect more deeply with my baby
- To feel what it is like to connect physically through the breast

- To give more of myself to my baby than last time
- To feed him breast milk so he did not get sick on formula (I got this in two ways: myself and non-stop donations!) In many ways the donor milk provided more advantages to him!
- To balance the dance of pumping, feeding, working, etc.
- To have the whole experience: breastfeeding in public, talking with friends, connecting with other moms about it
- To know that I gave it my all

In reflecting upon my seven-month adventure, I felt like I achieved everything. I finally decided it was time to close my journey for two reasons: 1) I was not able to produce more than one teaspoon a day, and 2) I felt that happy energy of accomplishment. I knew that despite not having a full supply of breast milk, I truly have been a breastfeeding mom and a success story!

CHAPTER 11

SUMMARY: THE MINDSET-ALLOWING-ACTION PROCESS

We have uncovered the processes and exercises which I used to allow my mindset shift to change from one of unworthiness and struggle to feelings of happiness and success. This chapter will summarize what has been presented to help you solidify your own path. Remember, there is no one right path for everyone. Presented is my approach to achieving something I really desire from any aspect of my life, and it allows me to experience my life fully and in a more relaxed way.

Coming into my full power means using all of these three areas together: mind, spirit, and body. They are in that order, too. First, the mind. The involvement of intentionally chosen thoughts sets the mind as the groundwork. If we were building a house, our thoughts (mindset) would be our foundation. I go throughout my day being aware of the feelings I'm having. When I feel a feeling which I don't like, or don't want to have, I ask myself, "What thought am I having that makes me feel this way?" and "How is this thought serving me?"

Awareness is half the battle. It is the ability to take a step back and separate ourselves from our current situation, just for a bit in order to analyze our thoughts, that brings us power. We have this cognitive ability, it just needs to be practiced! Our foundation of awareness and attention to thoughts which are purposeful lead us to emotions that better serve our goals. The change of our energy from reaction or inaction to intentional choice of thoughts will then permit vibrations (emotions) which allow us to feel our way forward to the next step.

Second, the spirit. Our emotion is the gatekeeper which allows (or disallows) the metaphysical to be involved. Call it the collective consciousness, the universe, unconditional love, God, higher power, or whatever label resonates with you. It is not hocus-pocus, nor some type of magic. It is our connection, and by using our emotional vibration, we align ourselves with the metaphysical. This connection (through feelings) gives us "feedback" in the form of perspectives to move forward. (Think of the F from the CTFAR model.)

Resisting vs. Allowing

We know if we are resisting or allowing our connection based on which emotion we are feeling. Positive emotions mean less or no resistance. Negative emotions mean we are resisting. Resistant beliefs (or negative emotions) must be let go because they hold us apart from receiving feelings of positivity, empowerment, and clarity. We can let go of them little by little, oftentimes by choosing an emotion that is just one spot higher up on Abraham-Hicks spiral of emotions (refer back to Figure 2 in Chapter 5) until we get to a neutral point. We also let them go when we meditate, because when we meditate

CHAPTER 11 — SUMMARY: THE MINDSET-ALLOWING-ACTION PROCESS

we drop all resistance. During meditation, there are no thoughts or feelings holding us back from our connection to our Higher Power.

Without resistance, we allow this connection, and a perspective comes forward. This is difficult to describe in words except by saying that it feels correct emotionally and logically. It is as if we begin to see the same world in a little bit differently as we "interpret," little by little, this new clarity we allow. It feels compelling and right. By contrast, with resistance, we block our paths from moving forward to permit clarity. We feel like we are banging our heads against a wall, perhaps. We feel confused, frustrated, angry, or any of the negative emotions.

Allowing unconditional love feels positive and light. For me, I feel how I feel when I am just appreciating the most beautiful song I have ever heard. The song speaks to my soul as I sit and enjoy. It feels great to listen to, and I don't feel compelled to judge it. I want to hear more. It feels like I am at ease, and I trust myself to enjoy and continue listening in my musical detachment. I feel secure — there's no real risk in listening to this song. This song is the right path of action to take and I know it by how I feel emotionally and rationally when I come across it.

***

Last, the body. The path or perspective comes forward; we trust ourselves to take it. We know it when we see it and we don't have the urge to question whether it is "the right one" or not. We begin to feel inspired to continue with it because we can't imagine why we wouldn't. (It is even beyond a feeling of motivation, because motivation involves a sense of cerebrally figuring out how to keep at it.) The new route feels helpful, supportive, loving, and in alignment to our desire. Even if it involves some hard work, we want to do it willingly because it feels productive and we are doing what we want. As we trust the perspective and path, we take action. Finally, our action brings success into our physical reality as we continue this process over and over.

I hope my description is helpful to you as you figure out your own personal direction to empowerment. A quick recap: using a strong mindset and thoughts which honor me allow me to tap into my spiritual side. Then, I take action from the physical side, because with my new perspective I feel compelled to take action to follow the new path I see. It is about working smarter, not working harder. I work in that order.

Here's my approach:

☞ Identify my feelings.

☞ Decide what feelings I *wish* to have if I am not feeling how I want to.

☞ Choose thoughts that permit those feelings.

☞ Practice these thoughts to grow the positive feelings.

☞ Allow myself to let go of resistance to how I believe it should happen. I believe solidly that it can happen for me and I let go of any insecurities of it not happening. This allows the universe (higher power, God, whatever) to start opening doors for me. It feels like circumstances start to change, but oftentimes it is that my frame of reference or importance regarding an idea is changing so I am seeing things that I didn't see before.

CHAPTER 11 — SUMMARY: THE MINDSET-ALLOWING-ACTION PROCESS

☞ Go about my day, in a positive mood... I start to uncover actions to take as they come to me. I know it when I see it because it feels good, and it logically makes sense to help me move forward. I can see how it connects and I want to take the action. I am inspired, not just motivated. I feel compelled to take the step because it feels right, even if it isn't one I have taken before.

☞ Continue with any step(s) as needed and appreciate each step of the process as it unfolds! It gets more and more exciting until the end result is final!

CHAPTER 12

LOVE TO ALL MAMMAS

I love all moms who are reading this book, no matter the leg of your journey you are on. You are a breastfeeding mamma. Whether this is your present reality, or you have regrets or stresses from your past, know that you are enough. Know that you have done enough. Know that all the decisions you need (or needed) to make were the best way you knew to love yourself at the time. Know that regrets don't serve you and the love you have with your child, and the current love you give is what is paramount. Know that you are loved, and you have the power and ability to feel that love whenever you allow it. Whenever you choose thoughts which permit feelings of unconditional love, you line up with the limitless energy of the universe and you are on your right path. It is your relaxed allowing that permits you to feel our Higher Power's deepest endless love; that love never has, and never will, go away.

I'm going to leave you with a quote from one of my favorite clips by Abraham-Hicks. She draws a picture for us of what being unwell is so we can better understand what well-being is. Imagine a cork bobbing on the water:

> Take hold of that cork and hold it under the water. That's you complaining about your mother, that's

you complaining that you're not making enough money. That's you, irritated that some condition has not lined up just right for you. That's you, misunderstanding your power. So you're holding the cork under the water — that's what negative emotion is, that's what resistance is, that's the unnecessary thing you've learned along your physical trail as you've been trying to find your way...[11] (Abraham-Hicks, 2015, 0:07–0:35).

If we could only stop holding ourselves underwater, we would learn that our cork is made to float automatically. This is the nature of our well-being: effortless, simple, and freeing. Gripping and controlling the outside circumstances of our lives will never make us deeply happy, nor will they change the outside permanently. Happiness finds us when first we allow our inside thoughts and feelings (whatever they may be), and then, if needed, exchange them for those which honor us and what we want.

Oftentimes a better question than "What would make me happy?" is "Why does this make me happy?" and "How can I find that happiness in an emotion first, before it manifests physically?" Then, our outside world begins to change. Life was a floating cork before we started to throw all our mistrust and conditions on it. It is time to let go of all the negative energy we expend by holding down our corks, and to allow ourselves to thrive! Cheers!

CHAPTER 13

MY FAVORITE RESOURCES

Below are some helpful websites and books. Some are specific to BFAR but most are not.

- Facebook page for this book! You can contact me here: www.facebook.com/I-Just-Cant-Fcking-Pump-Anymore-347094275985875/ or e-mail: mindsetshiftjohnson@gmail.com

- For BFAR moms, Diana West's book *Defining Your Own Success: Breastfeeding After Breast Reduction Surgery*. This includes a lot of practical information for making breastfeeding work for those who have had a reduction. Amazon: www.amazon.com/Defining-your-Own-Success-Breastfeeding/dp/0912500867 ISBN-13: 978-0912500867 or ISBN-10: 0912500867

- Medela Supplemental Nursing System®. This is a way to breastfeed your baby and not use a bottle. It can be filled with donor milk or formula to help supplement. www.medela.com/breastfeeding/products/feeding/supplemental-nursing-system

- Lact-Aid® nursing system. Similar to Medela SNS®, but a different brand. www.lact-aid.com

- BFAR Facebook Group which originated from Diana West's book.
www.facebook.com/groups/458224110894529/
or another:
www.facebook.com/groups/179939525406788/

- Free Podcasts from Brooke Castillo, creator of the Self Coaching Model. She has changed how I think about my life and empowers me to reach for better.
thelifecoachschool.com/podcasts/

- Brooke Castillo explaining the model herself:
www.youtube.com/watch?v=voi3TW_yytM

- Abraham (Esther) Hicks is a highly spiritual woman who channels the collective consciousness energy. This is not for everyone, but wow, does she have the love-centered perspective correct!
www.abraham-hicks.com
You can also find free YouTube videos of her sessions with clients.

- Downloadable Focus Wheel PDF mentioned earlier in this book: www.thevortex.me/wp-content/uploads/2012/12/focuswheel.pdf

- In need of donated breast milk? This is a free sharing site where you can post that you are in need or that you are a donor. FYI the milk is not regulated or tested, but many moms have even offered me proof that they are STD-free, etc. The

CHAPTER 13 — MY FAVORITE RESOURCES

group is called Human Milk 4 Human Babies (HM4HB). There is a Facebook group by state. Here is the national site: www.facebook.com/hm4hb/

- Eats on Feets is another milk donation site. This one also goes per state, but here is the national group: www.facebook.com/EatsOnFeetsHome/

- An Internationally Board-Certified Lactation Consultant is an invaluable tool. Find an IBCLC in the USA: uslca.org/resources/find-an-ibclc

- Find a doula for your birth. Here is one site, but simply Googling local results often works best: doulamatch.net

REFERENCES

[1] Castillo, B., The Life Coach School. "The Life Coach School Podcast Episode #26: The Self Coaching Model" [Video file] (2016, April 27). Retrieved from: www.youtube.com/watch?v=v0i3TW_yytM&t=1489s

[2] Rosenstein, S. "5 Easy Steps to Think Through Your Thoughts" *Suzy Rosenstein the Midlife Coach* [Blog Post] (2018, May 17). Retrieved from: suzyrosenstein.com/blog/5-easy-steps-to-think-through-your-thoughts/

[3] Alexandra, Leeor. "Abraham-Hicks' 17 Second Rule to Manifest Anything!" *Living Lovelee* [Blog Post] (2017, Sept 27). Retrieved from: livinglovelee.com/2017/09/27/17-second-rule/

[4] Abraham-Hicks, E. "Abraham-Hicks Opening of the Long Beach CA Workshop 2014-08-02 [Video file] (2014, Aug 5). Retrieved from: www.youtube.com/watch?v=WGI5GrPJBEY

[5] Hicks, E., & Hicks, J. *Ask and It Is Given: Learning to Manifest Your Desires* (Carlsbad, CA: Hay House Inc., 2004).

[6] Castillo, B. "What Is the Self Coaching Model?" The Life Coach School [PDF included] (2019, April 09). Retrieved from: thelifecoachschool.com/self-coaching-model/

[7] Davcevski, D. "Emotions, Frequency and Vibration" [Blog Post] (2013, April 10). Retrieved from: www.lifecoachcode.com/2013/04/10/best-3-emotions-frequency-and-vibration/

[8] Hurst, K. "What Is the Law of Attraction? Open Your Eyes to a World of Endless Possibilities" [Blog post] (2012, July 08). Retrieved from: www.thelawofattraction.com/what-is-the-law-of-attraction/

[9] The Nanticoke Indian Tribe. "The Tale of Two Wolves" Nanticoke Indian Association. Retrieved from: www.nanticokeindians.org/page/tale-of-two-wolves

[10] Abraham-Hicks [MyPositivityTeaCup]. "Abraham-Hicks – How to Do a Focus Wheel" [Video file] (2014, Aug 5). Retrieved from: www.youtube.com/watch?v=aEfEwp-_2Jk

[11] Abraham-Hicks (Phi). "Abraham-Hicks – A Cork Bobbing..." [Video file] (2015, Jan 2). Retrieved from: www.youtube.com/watch?v=e1LuX2S4Nro

ABOUT THE AUTHOR

Sarah Farrell Johnson lives in the Poconos, Pennsylvania with her husband, daughter, son, and pets. She enjoys her career as a French teacher and a mom. She received her B.S.Ed. from Bloomsburg University and her M.Ed. from Moravian College. Her passion is helping others; teaching is one way she shares that love, and writing is another. Sarah is proud to keep her maiden name as her middle name to honor her father who passed away from Lou Gehrig's Disease (ALS) in his early 50s.